P9-DVB-212

Hymn
for
Drum

Hymn for Drum

A Poem by

ROSANNE COGGESHALL

LOUISIANA STATE UNIVERSITY PRESS

Baton Rouge and London

Copyright © 1978 by Rosanne Coggeshall

Designer: Albert Crochet
Type face: VIP Palatino
Typesetter: Graphic World, Inc., St. Louis, Missouri
Printer and binder: Thomson-Shore, Dexter, Michigan

LIBRARY OF CONGRESS CATALOGING IN PUBLICATION DATA

Coggeshall, Rosanne, 1946–
    Hymn for drum.

    I. Title.
PS3553.04155H9   811'.5'4   77–28154
    ISBN 0–8071–0361–6
    ISBN 0–8071–0362–4 pbk.

"For John Berryman" previously appeared in *Caim* and
"Two Friends Make the Print" was first published in *Carolina Quarterly*.

In memory of Louisa Penn Ervin Howard

For Collin Drum Coggeshall
With much gratitude to my teachers:
Julia Randall
William Harmon
Louis D. Rubin, Jr.

Contents

BOOK ONE

Vacating

Prelude:
For John Berryman:
April 1972

For John Berryman
Thanks to WH

I

Two nights the dog has roomed in rain
   Beautiful & red.   Simple grow
The sleeves of this old shirt.
Dust forms windows in the floor.
Henry's book hurt   helped   is more.
Somewhere she is curling into sleep.
Not too rainy   Henry   not too deep.

II

Henry I have finished yr sad songs
& they are   mostly   sad
& songs   to here   around the wrinkle
Of a chord that grows a muscle
& is strong: chords of wrists reck
Blood & buckle into breath
That feathers flutes.
Show me someone sings
I show you bones what float.

But yr bones hit ice.
I wonder which broke first.
The sick grow lame in aim I think:
Sick. But only silver hacksaws tell.
I wall easily. Glass grows emptily
In twos   in threes   but   Henry
There are trees in the window
There are trees.

III

I never had a daughter   no.
But I drank laughter w/ my dog

3

Until she left   beautiful woman
Is her name   she's gone.
Rope hangs heavy in the hand
That hoops the rain.

Henry   I just opened yr sad songs
To say hello   goodbye   it is not so
Heavenly by impact for to die.

IV

Afterwards we all run out & cheer.
We take chalk & draw a polar bear
On that steep night.   They tell us:
Leave Henry Pussycat alone: he dead:
He deeper than the stone's lost blood.

We got no shoes   but songs are in our fists.
We all wear sweat like bandages & fly
     Oh Henry   we do fly with wings
& hold the hemisphere in spoons
     In saucers   cups.   No way is silence
Too unsaid to punctuate far praise.

V

Henry   now is like a gas gauge gone empty
     Lets us fill with slippery sleep
     Does not come when called   but   hid from
     Pounces   ravishes.   *Dream again*
Of the lost Maud suppling into fields.
Cellos play.   Somebody reads.
You are deader than the door my dog controlled.
I have welded all yr verbs into a wheel
That wasn't closed and won't
     Just rolls and rattles
     But it rattles sweet.

I can't let the letter die like this:
So unspoked   unholy.   Henry
     We are fully now a piece.
When I wear the shirt it has two holes.
Words are wells in which we drink or swim.
Their mirror skins hold rings for saving.
Ice does figure in.
Henry   I wd rather say
     Go cross the bridge.
The fatherest far is not too edge.

I
At Home: Rack Hall:
On & Off the Road

At Home: The Beginning
5/15/75

Him Cross pen be lost:
Irretrievable.

Nothing
In old house
Opens.

Ginny Mamadog snore
On him old quilt.
Rachel Puppy summer
Farther south.
No wet noses
Need him knees.

Easied by divorce
(C's   not him own)
He figure   still
Ol providence fuckup
Divinely inbetween & after.
Rilke-like he wonder:
"Killing true form
Of wandersorrow?"
(Him & others' own
He mean)

& he keep
Sweeping
Piling magazines
Kissing books
& looking
Under record   rug   & sheet
For him lost Cross.

II

Pen still lost:
Unrecoverable.

"If they ask" he say
(& nod they won't)
"I do need the drink."

> *To think*
> *Is worse*
> *Than*
> *Not to think*

"Who say that?
Mr. Bones' bones?
I got Luckies & matches
Aplenty
$ in the bank
& in the bunk
A Mamadog."

> *Lag in tempter*
> *Mix & meddle*
> *W/ the matter*
> *W/ it all.*

Years ago
(Just 7)
He give C
A wedding poem
About string & stone
Steps unstaken took.

> *Look back*
> *(Bones' bones advise)*
> *Be you prophet*
> *Or prop?*
> *Stop   look   & list*
> *Before*
> *You write a word.*

III

Cross   oh   lost:
Irredeemable.

& given him
By bestest friend
He never free.

Enfin (with apologies to Christine Brooke-Rose)

hallucinated lunch in the Speisesaal with persons
lounging gaseously concertina talk of tarot poems

when are they good when bad and etwas floats by
about how flying saucers on the plate smeared with

ideas of peupler le système solaire from spaceship
Earth con smitstof that likes to call itself umanità

while someone is it I keeps toiling up an Aztec
ziggurat toward the Pfarrer on the fork that slips

into the mouth of a spøgelse droning on about astrology
aber auf dem Tischtuch as the 747 vibrait uncannily

with a slow malrapide fastness violating chicken salad
a gross sebaceous Gesicht among les nuages suddenly

zooms personally me-ward like a fly and a stone knife
takes on the third dimension shooting ganz unerwartet

rasch straight for my pulpy heart as I sit futzing
with a beer and vaguely auskultis about tarot poems

when are they good when bad among the persons lounging
gaseously large and small in the underwater salle à manger

Fabula Morosa

Crow came down on the concrete coping
and hunched himself
and Squirrel whose wall it really was
made furiously

This blue sky opens wide like Jesus arms
the sun intones
after old manners and all that business
discourages me

So Squirrel chittered tail and teeth
and raced along
his wall but Crow sat lumpy and said Kra
and Squirrel fled

One proof of Paradise is not to die
go blow that

windily between your fractured fangs old
dandelion head

Flap flap went Crow toward the soft sun
squat Squirrel on
his wall peeled to himself a something
green reward

Let girls and boys go make together under
Jesus hanging skies
drawn onward by eternal murmuring of plum
Malvolio hears thunder

Stendhal Beyle Brûlard

and the two hundred other pseudonyms he took
to throw Linnaeus off the scent of his family:
wrote "imgo ingt obef if ty" in was it red
ink in the elastic band inside his trousers:

scribbled with his stick in sand the encoded
letters designating all the women he had loved:
by subscript indicating those he had possessed
once or twice in a life of endless perseverance:

detesting Paris he wanted to be buried elsewhere
under the insulting truth "Arrigo Beyle Milanese:
visse amo scrisse" but had to drop dead on a Paris
street and so was boneyarded in Père-Lachaise:

que voulez-vous, ce serait la dernière blague
for one who hated grocers priests and Sunday:
all that Grenoble blood drunk on memories of
horses flames snow emperors epaulettes and war:

and those reverberant soft velvet boudoirs of
the senses woman after woman mirroring enticement:
diffident fat provincial with a mind whenever he
could reach the goal he booked it in his diary

Satie

There is the inventor of the absinthe sandwich.
I have come to die with you he used to whisper
There is the matchbox Valhalla for the nightingales.
But in the end they had to come to die with him

There is the glass coffin gliding on a tricycle.
Opening his door for them by pulling on a rope
There is the fall of hammers auctioning his olive pits.
That ran over a pulley in the ceiling to his hand
There is the unsanitary belt of his old salty muse.
Where he sat like a rooster huddling eggs of pain.
There is the inventor of the humours of our evenings.

Dublin Poems

I   Aubade

As long as I have been sojourning in this city,
I have listened with pleasure to the crying
of its birds in the air: spooks or caretakers,
I cannot say which; perhaps even prophets.

I have watched them under all skies rising
high over chimneys, or bending toward the river
to rest on the rough stones of the parapets,
or floating into the pungent asparagus-broth

under the bridges, dipping for food. But only
once have I heard what I heard at five o'clock
one morning, bursting up out of my thicket
of dreams to run to the window to see

what bird could have uttered that death-cry
that had driven its beak through my eyelids.
I leaned out and listened: the cry was being
dragged up from green guts by a rusted hook

on a chain wound on a windlass. Was it because
it was ear-shy, or because it needed all
the strength it could get to tear itself out
through the slender spout of the neck? Whatever

the reason, that cry, already too dark
for the mind, seemed to be groining itself inward,
and to grow darker and thickly embedded,
like a car sunk in the silt of the river,

whose doll-jointed occupants sway as though
trying to help the grappling-hooks loosen them
lightward. I leaned far out and looked,
as far as I could see, into the damp dawn:

but found only a courtyard of blank bricks
and glass, half an orange face down on a skylight.
After a time, the crying loudly broke off,
and then tried to begin again, but couldn't.

II   Four Movements of Anna Liffey

1   *Chapelizod*

And on an unsettled day I climbed down from the bus
and walked a few hundred yards to the west past a church
and a pub, and, wheeling a corner downhill and downwind,
saw beyond the compacted roof-lines of a family of houses
long flattened hair of hillsides being combed green,
and came to what seemed like a bridge on which
I paused and leaned over and looked along the water,
which was dark and clean and responsive to the wind,
flowing alongside the houses, and I began taking pictures
but was doubtful, this water being so narrow, and when
a young man came by I asked him was this indeed the Liffey
and he told me yes and I said that it did not much
resemble itself when in town and he smiled and agreed
and went on, and I crossed to the upstream side
of the bridge and went on taking pictures of clarity
and of quick and fugitive movement, cold and dark
under low leaf-heavy trees, knowing it was really no use,
and then walked on a bit and turned back, sniffing clean air
and listening to the wind, and thinking how at this point
all was indeed innocence, and considering the influences
on the way to the sea that would turn this water of life
into slow supersaturated bile sumping between quays,
and how this dark child gaily unknowing would break
and run past Islandbridge and the weirs and past Heuston
only to come short up between in-closing sea-hairy arms.

2   *Ellis Quay*

At ebb tide this poor river has to confess itself
to a cloud-wrangled sky too busy to hear it.

A brownish-green oil draws down from the blackening
walls of the prison to which men have remanded it.

Limp seaweed overripe for the carding slumps in and out
of a quibble of upended prams and milk-bottle carriers.

By the big toe at the end of the curve of the bridge-foot
a sluice of something tawny undisturbs an eddy of gulls.

The cries of these birds rise with their white wings
as they manoeuver among rocks bared to the gums.

This water has been hemmed in for too many years,
and it faintly chafes as if it wanted to go somewhere else.

But the indifferent backhand of the sea keeps playing it
up and down along across the court defined by the quays.

And when the tide is at flood the black and green beards
of these walls are drowned in a coordinate trance.

Then the brownish-green oil stands up high in the bottle
wrinkling itself like the slow skin of an old man's face.

Opaque as a skin and resembling a syrup that brewers reject
this thick water repels the inquisitive visiting eye.

Which merely confirms that it must have something to hide
so that there is at no time any escape from confession.

All day a long march of dependable clouds takes place
while the river fluctuates between its high and low truths.

3   Sir John Rogerson's Quay

Along the grey quay-clatter the freighters roll slowly
and slowly yield like animals being unburdened or burdened.

The cranes riding their quadruped gantries dangle fat hooks
or if working swing and stop and swing again smoothly.

Here the river begins to become less sure of itself
for it is already turning into a finger of the sea probing.

Of a color as yet undecided it suffers the intrusions
of ships that enter it sperm-shaped and making long tracks.

On both flanks bounded it shifts as though obeying the will
of the man at a smudged window shortly docketing invoices.

There is bright blue slashed into its oleaginous green
but bright is still mainly for things men put paint on.

White meal of Snowcrete in bundles of sacks puffs out
as the claw of a crane climbs up from a low yellow belly.

And a thick man in a forklift angrily spears
a navy-grey barrel of stout and shuttles it eastward.

Another man in a forklift furiously pirouettes the barrel
to where a ship's winch raises and lowers it like an arm.

So concrete comes in and Guinness' goes out from Liverpool
to Liverpool in freighters crossing the wind-rubbed Moyle.

Or you might say just as well from Blackpool to Blackpool
since what goes on is exchange in the most literal sense.

Along an alphabet of stooping buildings a freshness is born
here at the slack mouth of her where she begins ending.

4   *The Pigeon House*

And as a last gift from the city she has to take in
a freshet of sewage creaming up like stout in the glass
from the outfall works just west of the Pigeon House,
and the tall stack letting off a brown feather of smoke,
but it no longer matters for by now she is very far gone
and altogether losing her self, and one way you can tell
is by the blueness and the skylarking of her under the wind
that blows up the big bags of clouds suddenly driving you
hard to the wall of a building for shelter from cold rain
that is over as violently as it came on, and commends
to the morning sun the patient roofs shining with wet,
and so when you ask about buses the young redheaded man
tells you no you can't go any farther and there aren't
many buses and "you better just trot on up the road now,"
tapping you on the shoulder as if to emphasize a sly point,
and the men clumped from the shower in the angle of a wall
come back out to their jackhammers, and as you turn back
breasting a tumult of air and delighting in on your right
the blue blue of the laxative Bay, a freighter glides past
and is gone to unload the oranges and apples from Sydney
and Jaffa you smelled the day before in Mary's Lane market
to be eaten by children whose pictures you took in Chapelizod,
and athwart the never-still empty wide water the shoreline
lies scrawled of the North Bull and Dollymount and farther
northeastward heavily low as befits the head of a giant
the wreathed Hill of Howth sleeps under burred shadow-lights.

III   Four Bagatelles

1   *A Sort of a Ballad*

The brown hair of the girls of this city runs down
    over their shoulders
but the water runs down over the lips of the locks
    of disused canals.

And wonder of wonders I saw on a wide morning of clouds
    two ancient swans
pick lice from their feathers where they were standing
    in the muck of the Dodder.

Beds of elaborate flowers are disposed in the gardens
    and the trees are green
but the color of walls in this city of walls is grey
    and even the sky makes a wall.

2   *An Apparition*

Riding the top of the bus on my way back
from Sandycove, I could not stop watching
a dropsical elderly man whose great head
kept falling forward into his arms
that hung like sacks over the top of the seat
in front of him, and french-fried fingers
he kept letting be scorched by a cigarette,
which would, for a moment, revive him.

To travel that way is dangerous, without
a mother to take it in and hide it
away from us, the waterlogged foetus
with adipose eyelids and undisciplined belly
that pouts like an underlip outward,
and a head that keeps falling forward
because, being in love with its toes,
it cannot bear to kiss them goodbye.

3   *A Vision*

Aimlessly walking the streets after having studied
at Charlemont House a show

of contemporary paintings, I felt an odd exultation
at this discovery—

four children's sandals without any feet in them, posed
pigeon-toed on the stones
of the pavement not far from the Communist bookshop
in Essex Street, and looking

as if they had been left there by a pair of ascending
putti, like those of whom
the chubby heads are stuck pertly through the ceiling
of the Rotunda Hospital

chapel, amused and indifferent and with an effect
of floating like gulls over
the Liffey, over the city, as if they could find nothing
below to warrant disclosing their bodies.

4   *Comment on a Comment*
for Ed Kessler

"Life," he said, "for me is an affair
of places not people": and there is
a beauty that can hardly be argued

in a street of shut doors and drawn blinds
on a morning of clouds, and nobody there,
only the bang of a bell in a steeple,
and a quick smell of coal-smoke, as if

someone sequestered had lifted the lid
off a kettle on an iron stove, and then
put it back, a witch behind gingerbread.

It seems all for a moment so spacious
without that slick feeling of eels
in a basket, but of course it is false,
and as a crowd of girls chatters out

of a convent, a street-sweeper shoving
his cart round the corner is passed
by an elderly cyclist winding himself

workward, and from behind a white
curtain, itself behind the glass of a tall
window set in a house built of brick, a hand
appears, gently watering flowers.

IV   Envoi

The music he was making sounded mostly for the eye,
a rude archaic body-language hammering out
the tousled swarthy truculence of those who, sagging
to their knees, keep struggling to hold themselves

upright, by help if necessary of the shoulder-blade
stone railing of O'Connell Bridge, into which
his backside-bones pressed, while his torso
swayed without stopping, to fro to fro, besotted

vagrant beast lumbering nowhere to the windings
of the drowned tunes his fists squeezed from the pleats.
Behind him, a long sun bummeled down into over
the Four Courts coiling clouds: and the river

breathed, up down up down, an exercise in prison
discipline. Before, melisma of green-and-yellow buses
underscored the evensong of workers eagering toward
a fanged mouth, six o'clock, gammon or plaice, potatoes,

in Palmerston, Stillorgan, Santry, Sutton, Castleknock,
and afterward the telly and the pub, suburb without end.
Nobody paid him any heed, no coins dropped flat
into the flyspecked box beside his brogues: he might

as well have been an eleemosynary singer, singing
only because not to sing would let death have the city,
or ratify the death already there in guise
of all that pullulation among dangerous buildings.

The fierceness in him was not just in his movements
but also in his voice, flattened at the poles, abrupt,
and surly as those are whose used-up bodies sense
and half-accept the fibrillated wounds of centuries

of life along the knife's edge: but even so secrete
a seedy pride that sends out shoots, grows fingers
of deceptive humor, continually opening and shutting,
slily murderous, around the ungovernable neck of history.

Dublin: June, 1972

Am I Not Your Son?

Years and years we met in silence after my Bible class,
and walked in silence to the drug store,
picked up the *Times* in silence, and in silence went home.

How peaceful and false the odor of your pipe—I too
by the way have taken to smoking now—
as you sat with your stiff back to the window's glare,

scanning and laying aside, methodically, section by
section, the Word of the world, until
the clock struck three, when you stood up, sighed, knocked

the ashes out, tuned in the Philharmonic, and put the water
on for the inevitable *Kaffeeklatsch*.
We practice lifting stones with forks of lead. . . . Old man,

old man, my father, listen to me now, even though your ears
are deaf, and we have so poor a tongue:
eighty-three years are vanished from your one sad life,

yet still you shuffle fearfully from mark to mark to mark
around the face of the gold watch your
father cursed you with, as if you might be late for dying.

Or is it that death, for you, was always the end of school?
But how am I to blame you that you claimed my *me*
where it sat puzzling itself among the uncompleted bones?

Some Realizations Come Suddenly

To hear a mind go, that is a frightening thing,
like watching a church being blown up in slow
motion, or as if a stone went rotten between
the fingers, and holes like pores appeared
and stared at you with angry eyes, as if
it was your fault that here comes crazy death!
Soft, too, like runny cheese, and those
abrupt discontinuities, how do you jump them?

The dwarf clown in the carny show, walking
head down across a muddy field or sitting
in a booth alone behind his untouched coke,
what would he tell the grandson he will never
have, when he is eighty-four, without his mask,

hating the spry birds flirting on the sill,
an eye in every one of his arthritic bones,
and the nurse comes in with the assembled lunch?

For many years I wadded up my mind against
my father's monologues about his past, his family,
the wealth and names and titles history
danced away with like a gay tornado, and now
that he is dead I have become like a museum
to him, noticing without surprise how I consult
his watch, write with his pen, and study out
the lineaments of all those portraits in my veins.

Requiem for a Persian. My Mother's Birthday.

Out walking on a Sunday afternoon,
the last in March, I stopped
because the grey-haired woman standing
at the extreme edge of her property
looked so angry, glaring at the street.
Behind her, two children slowly moved

across the lawn, carrying a makeshift
bier on which the cat lay, so I
was told, for at that distance
it was hard to see. Going silently
before, a third child, holding high
a sterling candelabrum, I was told,

borrowed for this one occasion
only, no doubt from the mahogany
sideboard in the dining-room.
The silver softly glowed. Three
specks of fire burned yellow
in the quiet air. The day was quiet

but overcast. Slow and solemn,
the children paced their yard, a mat
of brown just coming back to life,
and vanished around the house. He
was a Persian, I was told, four
years of age, eighteen pounds, prize

of a pure-bred litter, beautiful.
I listened to the children singing.

Whoever hit him was going over
the speed limit, not to be able or not
to care to stop, slow down, or even
swerve. People, I was told, are always

coming up that street too fast.
The woman's finger pointed. I turned
to look. The concrete, it was true,
was indeed smeared with a dull red
which might have been either blood or paint.
I had not noticed it before. From

behind the house, the children were
chanting something all together in a jumble.
Having buried, they now would mourn him. . . .
That Sunday was my mother's birthday.
I had just talked with her an hour
before. Her body's health, I understood,

was reasonably good, but she was cloudier
than ever in her mind. She kept
forgetting that it was her birthday,
confusing the ages of my children,
and could not remember when she last had
seen my wife. While my eyes remarked

that the red smears in the street were dry,
my mind smiled to think—but paint
would not so easily wash out with rain—
that my mother had already forgotten
both that I had remembered to call her up
and that she herself was truly eighty-four.

Graz, in the Summer of 1957

Night after night, in that moth month of August,
while your mother was elsewhere, I made you stories
        of Pedro Tavès, grand adventurer.
I lugged them up, slippery and green, out of the cold
undulations of my all-at-sea, and made them feasts

to stuff your gluttonous ears, which might have heard
unholy sounds. One night a mixed-up bat came whirling
        through the open window-dark.
We shooed him out again, a little scared, a little sad.
Pedro's career along the dusty highroads of the mind

was not for him, disoriented and minutely crying
the way a butterfly might beat and beat its wings, a
        butterfly burst from a fire.
A woman in a raincoat pasted hairs across the wood slats
of our coal bin down in the cellar, so as to find out

when Someone would remove the corpse she claimed was in
our trunk. Head down, she paced among the minefields
        when it rained, to tempt her enemies.
It was a hard time, what with microphones in light bulbs,
Russian bombers diving down upon the house, and agents

signaling between the hills by making windows lightly wink.
It ended when she walked with me to the white ward,
        the two-faced men, the insulin.
She did not know she was going there, but just before
we arrived, she wanted to sit down beside a pond

of floating ducks and grasses, where we drank two pale
mélanges at a table, under a pale sun of late July, and
        then went on, up to the end.
After that delivery, old Pedro Tavès, hero of my comic
strip, began, that ancient child, his brief engagement,

Don Punchinello in the mask of Parsifal, fumbling up
salvation tips from secret pockets, acting all the old
        pratfalls, all the usual escapes.
You and your sister turned into brats, that month, annoying
fussy ladies while I snipped the long path with my legs,

descending every queasy afternoon to reason with unreason
in the *Landeskrankenhaus*, although I could not comprehend,
        I, foreigner, its black patois.
And we, we sauntered among the trees at noon, and took
a table in the garden of the *Wirtshaus*, where you drank

Chabesade, and I dark beer, and all of us ate schnitzel,
Rotkraut, Rostkartoffeln. And in the end we went away. We
        could have stayed, but didn't.
I judged it pointless. So did Pedro Tavès, for he died.
I fished and fished, far down my all-at-sea, fingering

slick stones and old wet hairs, but there was no one.
Pedro had returned to the deeper country he had come from.
        We went away and did not look behind.
It was a time of bitterness and angry beds and wranglefear.
It lasted long: as long as the moment between death and death.

—Remember Pedro Tavès then, who rose and fell in one month,
whose raffish chronicle kept us alive among the stolid
    people, among the whirlingness,
Pedro, who scavenged for, and found, a kind of Grail. Remember
all your evenings the healing power of a foolish poem.

About That of Which One Cannot Speak, One Must Be Silent

The day of the eclipse, I took my daughter
to her small "rock park" down the street,
so as to find us each a proper station
from which to watch the woman moon of night
working to calm her husband's heat
by crossing him at just his fury's zenith.

I am no enemy to life, yet once I
scrupulously focused on a yellow spider
the German burning-glass my father
had given me for having done well in
arithmetic, until, quite stopped, eight legs
curled up around a shriveled belly.

Another time, beside the sea, stripped
to combustible and raunchy skin, in the soft
gullet of a dune, as shadows shrank away,
I drowsed, abandoned by the only one who
might have wakened me, so that I had to smolder
two weeks running on a solitary bed.

A little girl, head down, jumps carefully
among uneven, shadowed, spectral stones,
while an arrested man, his face up-tilted,
stained by a violet radiance in the sky,
warns her to look and not to look,
to keep a tree between her and the sun.

Are Roses Red in the Dark?

The stone lies at the bottom of the pool.

If a child, wandering by, should pause,
and stir the water with a broken stick,
aimlessly, as children will,

21

opening a round eye in a web of green,
the stone might seem to beat,
might seem
to beat like a dislocated heart
awakened to the feeling: once, I was alive.

There is the first dilemma of philosophy.
At most, we may propound: no toads are princes,
although some princes may be toads.
Why should a sleeping hand
keep opening and closing on itself?
A bequest of sunlight and clean air is called for.

In the end,
having lost interest,
flinging the broken stick into the tall grass,
the child, aimlessly, as children will,
would move away
through a soft rain of insects, while,
the round eye very slowly closing,
the water would grow still again.

And nothing would have happened to the stone.

Die Welt ist alles, was der Fall ist

If he still knows his name he has to
hang onto it with both hands clenched.
As a young boy I had to grip
the dripping sea-slimed rope
when waves came climbing toward me
on heavy mornings after storms,
and the bottom insidiously kept
changing shape between my toes.

Like a baby bird's, all trust and
hunger, his eyes expect from me.
—Are you the doctor, I throwed up
all my breakfast this morning,
must be I got stomach cancer.—
Out too far a yard and I would
start to slip down over my head.
I hated that salt water in my nose.

Open the screen door, walk down
the steps.—Gimme a quarter, I

Just sleep & send him out
For chockle bar each hour
Or so.

He fare for her then quit:
Sit on curbing & relate
To asphalt
How cleanly he shave by
Nonchockle BAR.
No car (not one   him own   or
Other) care to stop   & list
Or look.

He say: "Next book I pluck
From dust in shelf
Be book of hours:
6   8   10   12: strike:

Out
I get
The sweet
For Henriet'

Then
Beat
Mine tracks
Down to monky base
Where buttmountains topply
& cup & glasses
Be so wee
They only
Hold
One
Drop."

Grace
6/15/75

Him innersectum entranct from upbove:
Brother & his oner small
Come   thumpy   down
To gather round
Nowloud FM.

It make him hearty shake
To see how 3 be of a tree

(Familiar or not) so like:
A caterpillar tree?
A tree of cappylaries   branchy blood?

Oh good:
He wink back
Leapy tear.
Next year   this time   littlest one
Be 2: true: he thank
Him lucky stair

For

Giving way

To

Downy base.

Whim & Dream
6/16/75

I

Him whim:

Go call ol buster friend
& lend lost tongue to tell
How still a caterpillar tree
Can be late summer day

& say   then   how him nephew
Blow all a kiss & mess him hair
Into a crown

For friend so down
In drumless place
Where ashes steep
& reach each corner

White & drifty

Falling

All ways

Down.

II

Him dream:

Call lately summer night
& sieve no answer   no reverb.

This disturb & he begin a tap
On writerrung: old song brake in
(From low FM) & he again accuse:
"I too silly about the muse (sic):
It make me wrack & wreck
Mine only chair in half:
Now   room for 2 to sit:
But   admit   ain't none but one
Now under other weather
Where feather   pen   nor tapping
Touch.

Much   much   too feary & forlost
We wander   oh   a   part."

Ago
6/16/75

He come to one
Heartbreakt & bitten.
In steep wind him head
Go WHACK:

He burn table
Chairback   grave
In fire
W/(no)out look.

One take him whacky in
& hold old house:
2 gather & be founder
Of a newer guard.

It all   so   hard:
They lock him first:
They swallow key by key
Before him eye
Then lessen as he cry
& streak about how incesty
Lacks & losses be:
Of one kind:
Unkin but twinly   triply

Multiply
To pose & witness
Every blow
He take
In give.

When he leave
The wingy space
One piece him back
W/ strip & stare
    Forever sweeping up
Old stainy glass.

Never did one
Come (too) plain

& he
        Nonhelpfull
        To be heal
Still (& will)
Feel
For one
Who know
The rest.

Testy
6/20/75

He take (some fun)
A test in magazine
To show him "social power."

Henriet' appear to point
& slap her gainy thigh.
"I try" he fend "detrimining
Mine bend in matters
So shallowy inclind."

In key he find he be:
"Accepting": 23;
(Low: averagely);
"Enthusiastic": 10;
(Way below av.: thin:
"W/drawn" say key).

In "tact" (another page)

He score (he rage)
Bright high.

Henrietta look him
Eye to eye
& fist to fist:

"This best you ever do
In such: oh tacty   much
& much"   she glee.

He   scruffly   flee
& take long walk.
Rather not talk
Sociabul
Just yet.

Flight (Contemplative)
6/21/75

He write him boss in XYZ:
"Look here   less see:
I 3 years older now
Than whacko year
When me & tree
See eye to eye
&   moonylike   I muse
Unmuster of the fleet
In letter quest.
Here   I wrestly   quiet
(Unmurky place).
I see too clear
& have to say:
No way I walk the round
Xpound on litry matters
& do mine mutters
Too."

Oh true: Great Ax
May be in fall.
REjectory go strong.

& it a long
Long way
From where

He see
& where
Old arteree
Spurt
Reckony
Right
Word.

III
Missed: &/or Twisty Mail

Missed: &/or Twisty Mail
6/24/75

I

Doubly cross
He toss old pickle
At bin wall & huff   softlike.
No way out   w/ latches
      Catches   baby sleeping
      Henrietta locked in car.

He snuffle   dream of bar
In which he sit & sink.
Think unfriendly fakes
Back home be worser
Than him own low trek
Which net him nothing
Now.

II

"Look"   blasty   he rage to wall.
"I don't need all this cross
Understitchy fuss.
This long lowsome road
Be bendy.   Windyweather foe
Who know what time I slip
& where it break whenever
If I wake
Take liberality
W/ mine undergrownly heart."

He wish him twisty blood would break
Its bound & scree around dark mazes
Way it want.   He don't think he write
No more to them where he once live
& learn to burn deep letter of him name
In flame too low
To make a fire be blue.

III

Spin blue rage in sickly car:
Ride by bar   sniff   push peddle
Floorward & let go.
Henrietta know he mifft:
She sleep   or so she tend.
Him mind go windy as him wheel.
He squeal the long way round.
One bend he twist so stark
Him eye go dark in flight.

IV

Later
He return & cook
A fambly dish:
Wish every member well:
Take little oner by wet hand
& walk a walk.
No nessyscary talk:
Just walk old walk
W/ handy hand.

He bend him own free fingers back.
"Whacky" he remumble "better far
Than this.   Now mine head can read
What crossiness abound.   I ain't around.
Ones what left still go unreft
W/ airy waves.   They save inselves
Warm wicky lines.   Leave?   Not me.
Here   I be   but there   I see
Mine selfer 'sembling
    2nding dammed motions
    Missing in the past."

V

He write the letters:
One   another   4:
Upbove old squeaky floor
D-rupt   unspell him spilly pen:
"I lessen in mine base."
He hear him ownly word
Against still wall.
"I call & answer me:

Say: free to go;
Say: free to stay;
Say: day be darkest
When   where baby sleep
Still light slip   sudden   under-
Blind & bend around
Thin spokey crib."

Yesterday he rib him shadow
Out of bound & sing:
"I stick this round:
I wind old strand
Til it be straight
& drop   unweighty
Into water hole
To make
True circle
Widen
Into
Last."

History Lessen
6/27/75

He cover
Terrorstory
Of him past:
List name & number
Of survivors.

Initially   they spell
He see (& scree)
BEATME.

& off
He go
To tree
Where babe & he
Free caterpillar
Yesterday.

Now: night:
He nothing know
But stick

He throw
Another day
To scare
Fierce hound
Away.

No histreeantics
Now to make him play.
He whisk away
Small slip of fog
& stagger
Down
Where smoke
Be crown
& cuckold sign
Of every dam
He make
To break.

Small Song
6/28/75

Renumber one
Again
He sing to
In low night
Or high in gin.

Now
Him words
Wring down
& circle back:
Unwaxt.

Brief wick
He make
Go bleak:

It breaky

In

Him

Quick.

Toil & Trouble
6/30/75

In stew
He brew
Big pot
Of trouble:
Double drink
Of scotch
W/o one rock.

He like it fine:
It go down   hit space
Where spice of lift
Left   far   ago.

"Now" he mean he know
"Surviving in mine land
Be no matter of a show
Of hands."

Hanging Over
7/1/75

Pain
Mount
Down.

He draw
Small crown
On window
Of bent car.

Henrietta peek
& stare.   Say:
"Where been
Ol pen?"

"& you?"
He bluely 'cuse.

She choose
Compartmentdom
Again   & dive.

He walk   aloon:
Live & mixy
W/ close mucker air.
Him hair be wilder
Than her stare.

Underbone   he   ghosty   grin.
& he smoulder   smoulder   as he spin
Away.

Letterless
7/2/75

No mail
This morning train.
Absently   it brake
Him chain of thought.

Last night
He fought
Old Angel
W/ him fists:
He beat   he cuff
About cold wing & scale
But Angel win:
Again:
Like allways:
A. big boss.

So:
He live & well
In base.
He choose
A sunken book
& read
But head go racewise
Heart go whack.

Back in bluedom now
He don't know how
He wake or   worser   walk&talk
W/out a word writ down:
A stampy sign
From other   souther   way
Where

Him compass
Point
Right
Maddily
Today.

Torus: The Full
7/6/75

Read better day:
Him horrorskip say:
Change of addicthood
In sight.   Look right
& left you find
The mend be yours
To make.

It take him
Low & longly
To unbend
Old wound tin tunnel
Of him mind.
He find it give
Too easily   it take
To quick.

He smack him paw
& gnaw a letter
He rebelieve.
It drive him
Hartlike stuff
To stop

Stand   consider

& he figure
May   be
He   2   fools
In one.

IV
Ending: Weeks Pass

Weeks Pass
7/4–8/75

Him papa visit
    Feed him line
Heard on big fish boat:
"You are responsible
For any damage done
By   or in   your wake."

Him weak knee ache
& him whacky lid
Go rat   a tat   a rat.

It go like that a lot
These weeks (say 2)
Since who he be about
Come   doubtylike
    & stand   & stamp:

No good

Reading Henry's "He Resigns"
7/12/75

He read
The poem
Again
Tonight

& wait

& wait

& wait

For sleep.

Him lid keep rattling
&   between the knocks   he know:

Him   one   song
Gone   on   too   long.

He too feel resigny
    All   alone.

Then:
Stir&whir in head
    Say: "re-?" "sign?"

He line him eye
W/ eye of picture
On that book

& look

& look

& look.

Long Distant
7/12/75

So
He hum
Soft mmmmm
& dial
Long distant
Somewhere
He has
Never seen.

Wire too thin
To last or fasten
Word to word.
For openings
What do you do?

Closings
He find
Easier
Than pie.

Say:
"My   oh   my
    The pronoun
Cannot tie   or die
    Unknown."

Vermont: A Break
7/15/75

Today
He swim
Long way
From coast
In cold
New England
Lake.

He back
In element
Though grace
Be wasted
On him
Smokely lung.

In heavy head
He sing old song.
(Rumumble   all ways
    He float older
Than that song.)

He linger
In cold lake
W/ every guest

& list   too long
As names he notches
Wrestle w/ themselves
For
Him
Own
Air

He
Fear.

Flip
7/20/75

He   emptyhanded   hang around
Ol car w/ Henriet' & Hershey bar
At munch inside.

Him shadow longer
Than the tree
He see
Beyond.

Him darker head
Strike disappeary
As he watch it
Stick to ground
& turn around
    Around   around
To view
Who
Leaving
Now.

II

He free to go
    He guess.
He got him stick
    Him satchel & him sole
& holey shirt
Which bandage not
Him heart too well
It beaten so down
Low.

III

He toss a coin.
It show a head.
He know
It
Still

    Too still
To stay
Him own.

Con(found)fusion
7/21/75

In him mind   he find
A space
Where erasers play

For stakes
More steep
Than blood
Or beat of battery fist
On window pane.

Again   he sore   inside
Him cindered cell:
He make like hole
He carry in him shirt
Be all he call a tear

But
Under
Where
Bone   vein   & muscle touch
Be much unspoked & helly:

Waiting
For
The live
To move
& make
High way
Less twisty

More incurve

Of all
That round
& meet
To close

& form

A
Perfect
Sphere.

Lo/ast Letter
7/22/75

The letter   come   each day
Alone   & w/ its cover
Sever him sown heart.

He mutter   nightly
In him base
Less & less:
Mainly sleep
To keep old weaponry
In.

Gone thin   he snack
On butter bean from south
& bitter broth he   care-
Ful   hold in mouth.

Henrietta dead.
Or so he say.
No time to play
W/ selfmade ghosts
He guess.

He dress in dark
& work him way
Into a night
Where he may
See   to say
A prayer
More clear.

Coda: Vacating

Vacating
7/23/75

Him vacating all most done.
Weather bad: he breathe
Wet cloth & break in cough.

Him nephew fly
(In plane)
Away.

Enough:
Be said.

He   windowless   apart
Again must start   again
To move.

He live (be true)
Deep down
Far south.

Now even him own mouth
Make muddle of the word.

He hear
Tornadoes hit
Down there
Where
Soon
He sit

& count
The wrestings
He
Be left
To find.

BOOK TWO

Henrietta:
What a Miss

Prelude: Inhospital:
August 1975

Inhospital: I
8/10–20/75

Inhospital
As Henry 'plain
Ain't no great shake.

It tend to brake
All trainy thought
& mix the mustered verse
Into sock
In any jaw 'tall.

He know:
He stuck there
Once again:
10 daydrums round
This beat.

Round he go
& round he find
No thing
Resembling
A screen door:

No window w/out lock
In jawy strips
What line them:
Regularly.

Nurses' clanky shoes
Sport many newses of other impatients:

But he watch the watch
& count on him low FM.

At night
He   spiderlike
     Knit nets
& plea through window

In him door
For more than just another
Pacing shade.

He think   some   time
He strike to make a ship
In here   right now.
    But how?
Strip bedsheet?
Hook it to a book?
& bathtubs: here
They too confiney
    Too impact.
        No sea
Not even raintrimmed tree
Stick near enough
To touch
Or under stand.

So he back round
Them corners   veer
Away   in hall   from
Mendicanty door.
He wear him shoes all times

& want
& lose
A rime
To make
It
Right.

Here:
Night too steeply.
Day too bright.

Inhospital: II

Here he stay stuck again at 3 a.m.
Just lit another Lucky & the light
Still grin.

He done cite what prayer be left:
Now   drifty   count him toenails
Dream (oh wonder) where Henrietta be:
Free?   Fancy?   Dancing w/ them stars?

Several calls & no responser w/ right ringy word.
He figure he be heard   but not dare figure more.
So   slam him only door & wait a beat   wait two.
True: hospital rare & aromatic place
But him two faces still not seeing eye to eye.

He s'pose he maybe die in here:
Room so tomby   so cavecool.
He spect him tire be flatter
    Treadless   not rearing for to ride.

Up   he wander long & twisty halls.
Nobody calls & when he do it 'pear him self-
Er at another end   'sembling:
Crookt wires & crosst.

He   he know   he lost.
Still don't recall
Him last turn left.

I
At Home: Rack Hall:
He Begin Again the Count

Again: The Count
8/26/75

He begin   again   the count.
Alone   in him own rented Alcatraz
      He look out for seepy plug   lost cord
(Still connected   still lost)
Rays of sun that   simple   frame a bug.

Mother's mother's rug provide a porch
W/ steepingover room.
He feel he know each rimmy glass.
Quite slow he sip.
Fresh water go down breezy
Like a rain that will not fall
The morning after he sleep so soundless
He most forego the wake.

II

Wicked now he glisten
In him own (ungotten) track.
He stack old books   make a fortressy brigade.
Instead of wax   he lick all covers light.
At night he rumble through 6 or 7 rooms
      Answer echoes of himself & shake him silty head.

He know he dead some where:
Just can't recover quite the place.
So he keep on.   He wash him face
400 times & wait & wait & wait.

F(o)un(d)
8/26/75

Him Cross pen be refounded
In him own old changey pock'
& he wick around & jangle

He so please he jumpy out
Of skin & in again.

He live (he say) alone:
In 9 racket corners of him homely house
Dark spiders spin.
They just there:
He think he not permit them in:
They just there.
No eye do stare
Just long & langsome legs
What spin & speel.
They just there.

He know he pull pitch curtains
If he make a move toward lost.
It cast him 'bout aplenty.
He find he shut
Too noisely each ever' do'
& try to make a mend.

He do.
In come a friend
    Kindly show a face
    Erase them ashes
From him brow.
He begin to muse
    Again
    Of how
    (Now).

Night Music: For CC & the Red Clay Ramblers
8/26/75

He return again & hear tonight again the music
That first off framed him head & til it closed it shook:

Lost himself

In something other than the notes left or found
Unanswered or unread before a door closed too quick-
Ly &   all light   shut out.

Now he listen w/ the fan around him
& the dogdays leaving slowly w/ a promise
Here of fall—October—soon—next week

Perhaps   or just this last one month to go
Before he throw him message safely
Behind him
He be foundering a way.

For D
9/11/75

Each afternill
While sun silt

Down & under
Wakey trees
(Mostly plains
& fruity types what gnarling
Knicker at close roots)

He spy
Ol D's gray wheels.
Wonder twice if twice
Be still enough to stop
& go: not say so: not no:
Instead   he show this day
Be better far to stay & say
'Lo.

Time to Record
9/12/75

Since crown of thistles
Round him wrist
Remind him hourly
Of minutes he missing
When he too far turn him head
One way   he stay a while & play
W/ Mamadog   then work him legs
Into a walk what take him to a hard-
Ware sto'.

Don't stock no diaries
So he take him twisted hat
& leave: depart: enough
Of nails & chain mail
    Rope & locks & keys.

He hold a dollar
So he buy a drink—
A softly one in case
Of selfassault.

It all him fault he know
He break that glass
& end up in the other room.
"No broom to sweep" he remember:
Muse: "Not even now
        So may be best
If I forget
That record
Round
A while."

II
Downer South: The Ocean
Babe   & All

Colder: Time to Down on South
9/13/75

He ex-
Orcise
Him firey
Place:
Burn butts
Cremate envelopes
He lost
In purpose.

It bring good
Heat on changey
Day: season seem
Again to turn
& burning   he say
    Be this time
Of year.

Fire be quite
Respondy:
It lick up
Drop down
In way
He tell himself
He know
Be true.

It don't much
Have to do
W/ colding house:
Him rug be warm
Him sock be on.

It more to do
W/ underboney stuff.

Enough be hap-
Hazarding along
To mean him strong-
Er muscles must re-
Vert to weak.

Much be at stake:

He pile low log
Careful like it
Little timber
Too tender
To afford
A break.

It jump
In flame
Quite high:

Remind him why
& when him eye
Go watery
& him heart
Go whack.
He left
That yonker
In a northerly way
But now new letter say
(Though not received)
They all go way
To island beach
Where ocean breach
The floored' soul.

So
He cash
Him pay-
Ment check
& watch
& wail
A while.

Mailmany man
Toss in soon.
October fine
For beach pair:

Others
May take
A ride;
Hide them hands
Away.

The nephew be
Him only one.
He want to watch
(& show) the sun
Go down
Behind them

While the waves
Lick up
& back
& up again.

Small Trip
9/23/75

He take
Small trip
In trusty
True blue car.
It rabbitlike:
In fact it name
Flash Easter
& its heady lights
Quite right inside
Its squarey head.

It streak him
To deep lake
Where he were
Born (oh when)
& bled.

      Instead
Of shutters
All blue blinds
Flail wide:
Doors open
& the baby
In the grass

Grow more
Right now
The boy.

How fine
To glimpse
Them sturdy knees.
It pleases so
He begin a tape
& picture taking
Which seem to last
4 hours: it do: it true:
But intersectors interject
& interrupt & add a hum or 2.

Little oner scree
In mike & make
Red needle leap.
He feel he now afford
This lastest trip.
Him lap be mutterful
    Him voice be soft.

How can
In camera
With him weak eye
He born
A babe
So true:

The oner's size
Amazes:
        & "gracious"
Growner Collin
Glee today.

Tomorrow
He go by
In Rabbit
Car again

But

Like it say

It
Always
Re-
Appear.

Shackleford Banks: I
9/27/75

All music it seem
Turn southerly
W/ the wind   w/ the wind
Of him own stealthy path.

Finding no home
He hum   oh yeah
A hymn (long past)
& follow him own harey track.

Henrietta seek
In corners where he forget
To hide.   He hear her voice.
But.   Choice wrung in him
& he did her up: all right.

Tonight he sip from brother cup
     Look up & hope for star
He cannot in this hurricaney fog
Flee or look for.

CATASTROPHE:
Free as a bell he
But it pure hell
When ringer
Ain't around to pull
Him out & rock him side
Or
Even
Turn him inside
To
Sound.

Shackleford Banks: II
9/27/75

He sleep in him own childhooded room
A-part of dream of tendered days
When he walkt the beach watching out
For sills of ships   away   where
There seem no end of ocean   for old ocean
Internally impart   returnally depart
&   he know   :   it   all.

At 2 a.m. him nephew sleep across the house.
Little oner too this sunsplit afternoon
(A piece between two hurricanes) know no word
For eastward 'spanse of water what have as far
As he can see & be to tell no end.

Still   in chilledhooded room w/ low FM
He listen to new pocketwatchy tick.
He tack him toes w/ strips of old bondaids
& holler: H U R T.

He hang him shirt   sleeves out   in the wind-
Ow   for to die.   The membery of fambly home
In falling beach too hanger harsh:
Old music   old sea   go playing   true   & through.

III
Back: Falling in: Rack Hall

October 2 1975

In wide grin him lips be painted:
Face splayed   card played   table laid
For more than he do care to count.

Him favorite day   he say   hooray around
    Harrumscarrum   buying up tickets   giving out flags
    Calling up all clowns to bear him downs   & ups.

It all amass to this: he find him homely house
Stay shaded   even in the day.   Cold chime in:
Oh whack.   He seek for stick for spirey place:
Find none.   Run stark raving naked through him door
For paper (news- or anyother work) to ball up quick
& toss into blue flame.

He write him name on stickless envelopes.
Send out blank posters what bear dimensions of him-
Self: size   shape   & time of day he shave by.
Posters never read: WANTED.   Or   even: WANT.
Posters read: WILL.   WILL.   PLEASE.

For Stephen Tapscott & Susan Tarrant
10/2/75

I

Mail motion in with wringer book
From friend in far midwest.
It buster book! of poems & peaces!
Places he once be & see & know
About 5 years!

As well of folks
Whose hands he misst or shook!

Taking long look
He shake dark fally locks:

Nick him throat   knock him
Better mood to mist.

II

For low long time not hear from bufferfolk.
Still & yet old reason drum
On in & friend come
Back w/ wife
(Him friend in deed).

Both do keep calls (in need)
Understand how falls mount up:
Sometimes explode:
How leaves be all some times
There be
To forest   field   or any fold
Of day.

III

Tonight in honor of young poet & wife
He play a song & two.   Music carry
Even when phone wiles
Do fail to quite converge.

No emergency: not now:
Him house struck cold
But doors & windows open
Either way & him bunk blank
Be   oh   new & fine.
(Fr Bean).

For F: Moon Song
10/2/75

A voice   a song   about the moon   he hear:
How harsh be   old mystery.

It fallen day: October winds & blesses:
Breezes bring leaves   quite bright   too new
To be as old as all this.

Missing again he pass old bar
    Pat him rabbit car & mill on Henrietta
In him gravest thought.
Although he bought her all the chocolate

In Mass   still   she wd not partake in speech:
Not come out & move to say: "hello" "goodbye"
"How come you never cry no more?"

He do: he know: but how to show
Him hearsted friend?
Him band bent ragged:
He one man show (so so)
But can't go on for never.   No.

Or can he?
No October soul fills full him questing track.
2   many   backs torn   too many cuts run rugged
In him trail.   He wd tell her now a thing or 2:
All true: far as he stay able now to plea.

It entale a splice of love: brotherly & un:
He do wish the monk & nun not come to call
So often to bring fire &   for him hearth
Twicetoasted marrowbone.

He misbegetted many nouns   a verb or 6 since May.
Now he beg for sticks   small timber to intend him fire.
W/ him chippy shoulder sore now it colder:
Now he want more than rings & water
    Birds & bleeds.

Deliverance
10/5/75

He pull   at least   an all night drunk:
He think it fine at time but wake
W/ broke in head & waded water
All about him boots.   He let him hair
Go down from bed   wish he dip dead
& spy   instead of rug   goose bug
W/ feather in it beak.
It clack about   it speak to him:
"Drunk don't do: carry wisties through
For just a time but old dime don't fit
In single slot & can't connect the call
W/ one you want at all an answer from."

Not interduced he flash back
& feel him knickers all aflail.
He walk about & wail & wall him socks
Far in.

"Don't touch" he beg old Mamadog.
"Leg do hurt & head do whack."

Don't think he recognize no answerer;
Just empty him deep pockets for relief
& watch old leafs stack up:
Cup after cup   on bottle   bottle.

"Must settle down" he sigh   sighing.
Must mettle round he see.
But   still   he plea: oh why?

No Dream
10/9/75

Night pass it seem:
& no dream visit
Or stick round or steer in window
& snuffle up respond.

So he just lay out him graver clothes
& strut unwieldy all about the rim
Of him old cobweb household where
Him friends once crosst   oh many paths
& stuck   some times   to change
Them winks or tunes or tires.

He say: "Sleep come on too easy.
I curling into ringside seat
& then no show   not one boat
    Dream- or other kind
To winkle seam in mine ownly eye.
It too much like I go that far
To die each night: a slip of cooler
Water & the pill what stills."

"Hmmf" he want Henrietta there to say:
"Day must be met.   Must get
Them Papermates tolling in your class."

Still he fret he pass too quick
These every night what come up so slow
& settle down & hold: pills still:
They loosen him   then come in   wolflike
    For the regulated kill.

Plan to Purchase
10/9/75

When he have the time he sit in smoke
(Short Lucky) & hum a little hum
'Bout what come & go   like smoke   or steam.

He mull: "I purchase some time drum;
Drum & punchy bag.   Then I need not swig
This Crush or chomp this Hersheyette.

Henrietta   please   come back."

Invitation to a Spider
10/11/75

"All birds be folded down.
 I choose a crown of cufflinks
 For my hair   curl on my bunk
 & sink about the Sunday day
 What follow this.
 I hide my Cross:
 Stretch bare & open to unleash.
 My wish wish me   & still: no show."

Brown spider riddle up him arm.
He say: "Bite.   Alright.
I sicken & I die & may be
That be the lie
That bring her up again."

But he remumble when & how
Him threat no longer work.
He lark about the yard:
He whistle & he snark
But it go dusked' dark
& still: .
       No Henrietta compromise.

"Next shift" he brave
"I wax unarmied   w/out blue pill
      Mine drink   or even that mine sweet-
   Est Ginnydog to take the task.

The only thing I big enough to ask
Be this   (& not a prayer)
That when   whenever next I wake to wake

Some single sign

Of her
Be there."

Aging
10/11/75

Looking
At him leafface
Turtleback hand:
Steadyish
He determine
To miss
Not a single slip
Of fall.

A little ditty hum
Think a willy thought
He bet he think
When no taller than a drum.

"Somewhere
They kill blue albatross"
He muse.
But it confuse him own left tongue.
He want him younger self
To re-emerge   take Henrietta
By the hand & reconcile.

"I ain't no child" he re-collect.
"But expect mine year shoot
Longer than H papa gun.

I find a one to walk w/
On another fallen day.
Just a matter
Of what to mutter
& what   in felt   to pay."

Portable
10/11/75

"I live very portable"
He muse as he meander
Through the field.
"Called nomad I be no-
Thing more: but w/out
    Of course   the no.
I suggest my falls
Too willfully   they say.
Win or lose   must titrate.

Don't mean to bruise
No other body's failings
But can't help come on
Too long too strong
To last this time of year."

He take a swig
    Bend down
    Re-tie him hikey shoe.
He dresst in blue
& blue he flee.

Now he free to wander
Any wood at all
He fear   all ways
He miss the seventh call.

IV
Come Christmas & Whateveraftermath
There Be

Christmas Coming
12/23/75

He
So
Down
Low
Even
Knee
Of tree
Too
Tall
To
Touch.

He
Go
About
About
At look
For
Some thing
Like
A sign

But
No thing
Move
No thing
Give

Even
Lovely son
Of brother
In far north
Admit

No commerce
No exchange
Of hi's
Of 'lo's

Christmas 1975

All him holing
Into darkness
Giving
No relief:

Undercover
He stick still
To peep:
"I as well as donefor
With my hat lost
My other shoes in hock.
Sick I am of moving out
Looking for a light.
I just as soon go down
The third & lastest.
I lost the only mirrorimage
Of my self's light side:

Gone away
& with it took
The shadow
My hands could make
When reaching
Upwards

Meeting

Making air
A prayer."

He Wake
1/1/76

Not morning:
Night still hang.

He sip a toddy
Slip a noose

About him neck
& bet him shadow
He not last til noon.

"She gone" he moan
"& I the one
Who triggered
Her last looking
Out of scene.

"I been
So low
So long
I think I swing
The hatchet
    Kick the pail
    Ride the rail
To down
Where ghosts survive:

She live too open
For my mind
& I be blind
To overlook
How like a swine
I been
When I pushed her
Into gone."

Two Friends Make the Print
for Stephen & Myra
1/6/76

I

He read 2 books
At once
    Rung about
By wicky friends
Who live in distance
Coming close
When him thought
Turn under
Wondering at wind.

Good words wend in

Lend him season of plenty
Not a bit like creeping low-
Ly years what tamp.

II

"I recognize
These limber lookers
Who hook words
Just so
To let all others know
There is a morning train
What leaves the knocks
Behind."

He stamp & swear.
Wish he be there
Beside the station
    Waving at the fireman
    Leaving for the wide
Wondered places
Where they fix them words
    Twist them phrases
Into praises
& silk prayer.

Lost: Grand
1/22/76

He come in to stomp
The phonelow ring
& lean   back in him shade
Because they say she dead
    The one who give him time
& teach him heart to trump
No matter what the threat.

"Can't let her go"
He mutter.   "Not like this.
Must watch them hearses
Herding in   black bullets
In my slivered chest.
She be first & best
Within the cycleframe
My roomy life.

Now I lift my prayer
   Little tattered sleeve
& let the upperstories know
I never loved like this
   So spacious & so fine
That I tear
To let that ghost give in."

Wanted
2/2/76

He wake   open letters
W/ him toes & find
He wanted in 7 places
Undersun.

In Albuquerque specially
They want him face
For proof of life
Presuming after breath
Be lost.

He refuse each query
   Open up some crackerjacks
& eat the prize.

Houdini
2/4/76

"Call me Houdini" he say
"I muck around the marker
   Kick away the dirt
   Unlock the locks
   Untwist the chains
   Release myself
Still squinting.

"I tempt every way I know
To lose this brittle body-
Shape I move.   I wave
   I say goodbye   & when I turn
I spy it coming back behind me.
If   tomorrow   you miss my knock

Don't try to find me.
When she left I figure I go too

But

It a far far simpler thing to do
To scape what you want to keep
Than to leave the face
They say you're born to bear

Each morning
Through the baffled air."

Open Window
2/7/76

Today he bring home bacon
    Wash him plate & proceed
To wait.

Surely a ring rending winding
Round him unholpful ear
What list & list
& long & long.

"I ain't got string enough
To hang this lesson out"
He 'low & leave on northbound bus
For land afar what got no name.

Now: no whim:
Simple stark un-
Ravelled pain.
It begin to swim him mind
    Make waves unruly
    Waking him all nights
To single sheets
& the window he forget
    To shut.

Flame: Dream
2/12/76

He watch beside the fire
Old dip & doffle of blue flame.

"If mine ownly hymn do breathe
Of new" he mull "I draw
Horizons on my pockets
    Build a truer guard
For Berryman & Yeats
    Relax the torsion in my chest
& fist another decade through."

He live these days
For 2 blue firers:
One: the twinning of him dream:
Ol Henrietta up & out;
The other: him wet dog-
Eared clown what snark around
& give him shin a lick
When he so pained
He find he have to kick.

Complaint
2/26/76

"I live nowdays inside a blue tall well:
A circus tent: it twenty mile from there . . .

"It too easy to complain   admit   you got
To take your bit & settle down: she gone."
He whisper to himselfer words what wonder
Where they been: thin lines of resignation:
Notice of *no give*.

"Outside a sycamore at night become a door
To higher me to her who left me   windows
Down   pants stringing on long line   no lickerlist.

"Now in rings I go w/out my shirt.
Lifting my fingers into stars
I cry 'where my fortunate spurs?'"

True or False
3/1/76

Rebroken
From the cave of air
Where she been   cagey

Hiding out for months
She grin   "How do ol boat?"

He catch him throat & stifle
A small scream: "You resurrect
Your ornery self?" he cry
    Afraid again he may mistake her
Voice.

"Your loss is now again" she give.

So steep to see her live
He grab her hands
& do a little dance.
She whirl & step.
He 'form her she him weapon
Up gainst an early spring.
He bring her Nestles crunch & coke.
She eat & drink—
He got to figure
    This no choke.

Coda: Henrietta

Henrietta
3/3/76

Four at a time she come
Down the stair she so joyous
To be free & trusty
    Guardian of wings.

Often now she sing & pirouette:
Let him watch her if he pay
W/ gloves   chocolate   or soap.

"I just happen to be a gracelike waif"
She croon "I make small tracks
W/ twinkly blossomies for toes.
I free   ol bone.   & you?"

He know no answer
So he twist about
    Look down   & frown.
Ash Wednesday   day:
He discover nothing stay
    Less it touch him crooked wrist.

Can't pray   so stay & watch
Henrietta dance & play.
She so angellike in her true duds
He feel him heart stand up:

She anything
He ever have
To lose.